creatures of the sea

Dolphins

Other titles in the series:

creatures of the sea

Dolphins

Kris Hirschmann

KIDHAVEN
PRESS™

THOMSON

GALE

San Diego • Detroit • New York • San Francisco • Cleveland
New Haven, Conn. • Waterville, Maine • London • Munich

For more information, contact
KidHaven Press
27500 Drake Rd.
Farmington Hills, MI 48331-3535
Or you can visit our Internet site at http://www.gale.com

LIBRARY OF CONGRESS CATALOGING-IN-PUBLICATION DATA

Hirschmann, Kris, 1967-
 Dolphins / by Kris Hirschmann.
  p. cm. — (Creatures of the sea)
 Summary: Describes the physical characteristics, behavior, predators,and life cycle
of the dolphin.
 Includes bibliographical references (p   ).
 ISBN 0-7377-1555-3 (Hardback : alk. paper)
 1. Dolphins—Juvenile literature. [1. Dolphins.] I. Title.
QL737.C432H58 2004
599.53—dc22

                                                    2003015038

Printed in China

Table of Contents

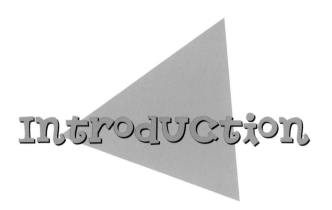

Introduction

Natural Acrobats

Dolphins are among the ocean's most acrobatic animals. These powerful creatures are known for their ability to leap far above the water. Wild dolphins often fling themselves upward in a behavior called **breaching**. Breaching usually carries dolphins just a few feet above the water's surface, but more spectacular leaps sometimes occur. Scientists watched one dolphin catapult its body more than fifteen feet into the air before splashing back into the ocean.

Some dolphins can do even more amazing things. Common dolphins, striped dolphins, and many other species do somersaults in midair. Sometimes these dolphins do many somersaults in a row,

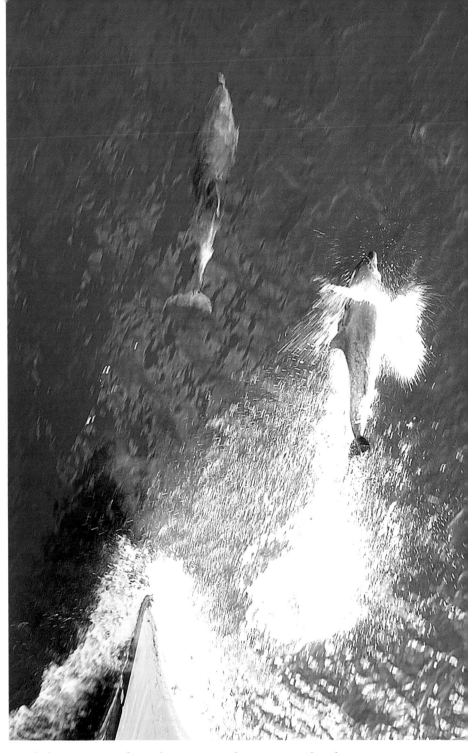

Dolphins can often be seen playing in the bow waves of ships.

one immediately following another. Another type of dolphin, the spinner, has an even more impressive ability. It twists sharply as it leaves the water to spin its body. The dolphin corkscrews through the air, making as many as seven complete rotations before dropping back into the sea.

Dolphins use their athletic abilities to help them ride ships' bow waves (waves pushed in front of a ship as it moves forward). Several dolphins might travel with a ship for miles, sliding along the bow wave and jumping from the water over and over again. Sometimes dolphins are even seen riding the bow waves of large whales. They also "body surf" on coastal waves, letting the water carry them close to shore before turning back to sea.

Marine parks give the public a small glimpse of dolphins' physical abilities. In these parks dolphins are trained to leap high in the air, do somersaults, "tail walk" across the water's surface, and perform many other stunts on command. These tricks are impressive—but they are also completely natural. Wild dolphins do these things all the time. The main "trick" a theme-park dolphin learns is how to follow a human command. The stunt itself, whatever it may be, is second nature to this incredible acrobat.

1

Ocean Torpedoes

Dolphins belong to the scientific order *Cetacea*, which includes all whales, dolphins, and porpoises. Within this order, dolphins are included in the subgroup *Odontoceti*, which means toothed whales. The toothed whale group also includes beaked whales, narwhals, sperm whales, and porpoises.

There are thirty-eight species of dolphins. Familiar species include the bottlenose, spinner, spotted, and common dolphins. Some small whales, including killer whales, pilot whales, and melon-headed whales, also belong to the dolphin family.

Dolphins are not fish. They are **marine mammals**. This means they have warm blood and breathe air, like land animals, instead of having cold blood and breathing water, like fish.

Dolphin Bodies

Dolphins come in a range of sizes. Several small species, including the black dolphin of Chile and the Hector's dolphin of New Zealand, measure just five feet from nose to tail. The largest species is the orca, or killer whale, which may grow to more than thirty feet in length and may weigh more than eight tons (sixteen thousand pounds). In all species, fully grown males are larger than females.

Whatever their size, all dolphins have torpedo-shaped bodies covered in smooth, sleek skin. The skin color varies from species to species. Some dolphins are a single color all over. Others have gray,

Dolphins are classified as marine mammals. The bottlenose dolphin (pictured) is one of thirty-eight dolphin species.

black, tan, white, or pink areas. One species, the spotted dolphin, has spots all over its body. Several species have stripes.

At the front of the body is the dolphin's head, which is tipped with a visible **beak**. The beak includes the dolphin's mouth. In some species the mouth is curved up at the ends, giving the dolphin a permanent "grin."

Just behind and to the bottom of the head are two **pectoral flippers**. The flippers are stiff, flat pads that contain bones and cartilage. A dolphin cannot move the bones within each flipper, but it can wave an entire flipper as one piece. The dolphin uses its flippers to steer as it swims through the water.

Standing up from the back of most dolphins is a triangular **dorsal fin**. The dorsal fin keeps the dolphin from tipping over as it swims. Some dolphins do not have dorsal fins, however, so this feature probably is not essential to a dolphin's balance.

Behind the dorsal fin, the dolphin's sleek body narrows to a flat tail with two lobes called **flukes**. Flukes are flat pads of tissue that contain no bone or muscle. A dolphin waves its flukes up and down to push itself through the water.

Adapted to Ocean Life

Like all mammals, dolphins must breathe air. A dolphin breathes through a single hole on top of its head. This hole is called the **blowhole**. When a dolphin is underwater, it closes the blowhole by covering it with a muscular flap of skin. When the dolphin wants to breathe, it comes to the surface and sticks its blowhole out of the water. It relaxes its flap and blows out old, stale air. Then the dolphin sucks in a deep breath of fresh air. It closes its flap and dives back underwater.

A dolphin near the surface breathes several times per minute. A diving dolphin, however, can hold its breath for ten minutes or even more. The dolphin can do this partly because its heart rate drops dramatically. A slower heart rate helps the dolphin to burn less oxygen, so it needs less air and can stay underwater longer.

Staying Warm

As marine mammals, dolphins have special features that help them to stay warm. A dolphin must keep its body temperature between 96 and 98 degrees Fahrenheit (slightly cooler than the normal human temperature of 98.6 degrees). For this purpose, dolphins have a thick layer of fat called **blubber** just beneath their skin. The blubber layer traps the dolphin's body heat and stops it from escaping into the water. Also, blood vessels in the dolphin's flippers, flukes, and dorsal fin can get wider or thinner in response to changing ocean temperatures. When the blood vessels are wider, more blood flows near the skin surface, and body heat

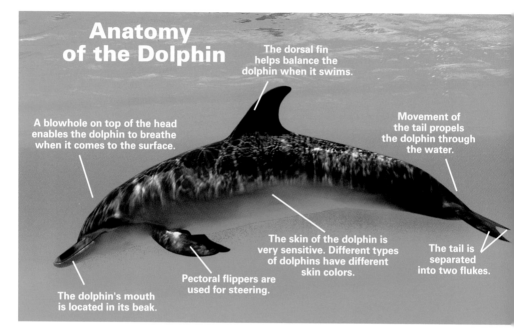

Anatomy of the Dolphin

The dorsal fin helps balance the dolphin when it swims.

A blowhole on top of the head enables the dolphin to breathe when it comes to the surface.

Movement of the tail propels the dolphin through the water.

The skin of the dolphin is very sensitive. Different types of dolphins have different skin colors.

The tail is separated into two flukes.

Pectoral flippers are used for steering.

The dolphin's mouth is located in its beak.

escapes into the water. When the vessels are thinner, less blood reaches the skin surface, and very little heat gets away.

Echolocation

To get around in their ocean homes, dolphins depend mainly on an ability called **echolocation**. Echolocation is a built-in form of sonar. It lets dolphins "see" objects and animals through sound instead of vision.

To echolocate, a dolphin makes a fast series of clicking sounds. It sends these clicks through the **melon**, which is an oil-filled organ inside the dolphin's forehead. The dolphin changes the shape of the melon to focus the clicks into a tight sound

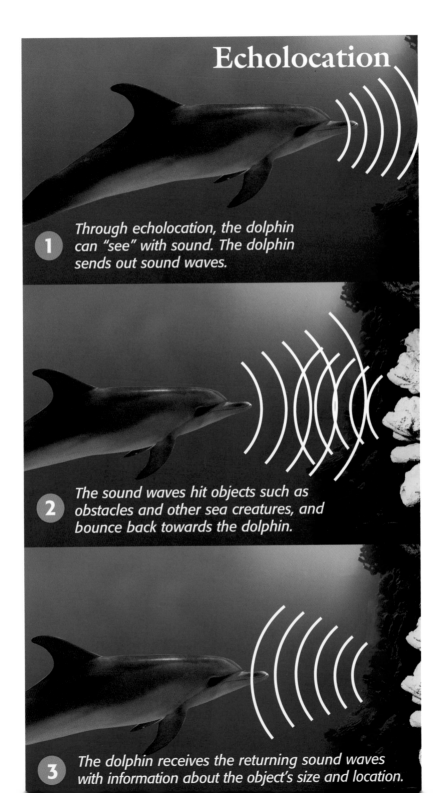

Echolocation

1 Through echolocation, the dolphin can "see" with sound. The dolphin sends out sound waves.

2 The sound waves hit objects such as obstacles and other sea creatures, and bounce back towards the dolphin.

3 The dolphin receives the returning sound waves with information about the object's size and location.

beam. This beam shoots out in front of the dolphin and bounces off objects. Echoes then return to the dolphin, where they are picked up by the fat-filled lower jawbone. The echoes pass to the dolphin's inner ears and then to the brain.

Inside the brain, the echoes are translated into information. The translation is based on many factors. The amount of time it took the echo to return, for instance, tells the dolphin about an object's distance. Tiny differences between the original clicks and the echoes provide information about an object's shape, texture, and motions. Taken together, these bits of information can tell a dolphin whether a distant object is a tasty fish or a piece of coral. Echoes therefore let the dolphin "look at" boats, the ocean floor, shorelines, floating chunks of ice, other dolphins, and anything else in its environment.

Other Senses

Dolphins use sound for more than just echolocation. They also use it to communicate with other dolphins. Clicks, squeals, whistles, grunts, and other noises are produced by air sacs inside the head, then sent out through the melon. These sounds are a dolphin's "language." They provide information about a dolphin's location, mood, and identity. They might also alert other dolphins to dangerous situations or food sources.

Dolphins have excellent vision, and can see underwater much more clearly than humans can.

Sight is also important to dolphins. Dolphins have excellent vision both in and out of the water. Also, their eyes can adjust quickly to dim or bright light. This ability helps dolphins to see as they move between deep, dark waters and the sunny ocean surface.

Dolphins also use the senses of touch and taste in their everyday life. A dolphin feels the world with its sensitive skin, and it tastes with its large, humanlike tongue. Like hearing and vision, these senses give the dolphin important information about its world.

The one sense dolphins do not use is smell. This sense is not important to an animal that holds its breath most of the time. Dolphins do just fine by relying on their other senses instead.

2

The Dolphin Way of Life

Dolphins can be found in every ocean of the world. Some types, including the hourglass dolphin and the killer whale, roam the cold waters near the earth's poles. Most dolphins, however, prefer the warm waters near the equator or the temperate (cool but not cold) waters just above and below the equator.

Some types of dolphins are very common around the world. Bottlenose dolphins, for example, can be found along most of the earth's coastal areas, and common dolphins live in warm waters everywhere. Other dolphins have smaller ranges. Commerson's and Peale's dolphins, for instance, live only near the southern tip of South America.

Bottlenose dolphins can be found in most of the earth's coastal waters.

Living Conditions

Different types of dolphins prefer different living conditions. Some species, such as the Irrawaddy dolphin of northern Australasia and southern Asia, stay in shallow coastal waters throughout their lives. Others, such as the Risso's dolphin, spend all their time far from land. And some species, such as the spinner dolphin, the dusky dolphin, and the common dolphin, can be found in both shallow and deep waters.

Some coastal dolphins stick to a small home territory throughout their lives. Most dolphins, however, travel around during their lifetimes. Some types of dolphins move randomly, following their food sources wherever they go. Others make seasonal **migrations**. This means they move back and forth between two specific home areas at the same times each year.

Sticking Together

Whatever conditions they prefer, all dolphins have one thing in common: They are almost never found alone. Dolphins of all types travel in groups called **pods**. Some species, such as Hector's dolphins, form small pods containing just a few animals. Other species gather in huge groups. Fraser's dolphins, which live along the Pacific equator, form pods of five hundred or more. And spinner dolphins, which are found in warm and temperate waters around the world, may form pods of more than one thousand members.

Within their pods, dolphins are very social. They chatter constantly and respond to each other's "speech." They swim close to each other, touching and rubbing with their flippers, beaks, and flukes. Dolphins also recognize each other, and they often form strong preferences for specific pod mates. Dolphins who bond in this way may stick together throughout their lives.

Life in the pod is not trouble free. Dolphins have a strict social order based mostly on size and strength. Big, strong dolphins (usually males) are dominant, and they will fight with other dolphins if they try to take control. To show aggression, a dolphin might smack its tail on the water's surface. It might also bite or scratch another dolphin with its teeth. Most adult dolphins have tooth marks on their skin, which leads scientists to think this behavior is probably very common.

Still, fighting is the exception among dolphins. Most of the time these animals live peacefully together. They also cooperate and work to keep each other safe. If a dolphin gets sick and starts to sink, for example, other dolphins may push it to the surface over and over again so it can breathe. They take turns doing this until the sick dolphin either gets better or dies.

Mating and Birth

One important function of the pod is to provide mating partners. In some tropical species, mating takes place throughout the year. Other species mate only at certain times of the year.

Dolphins show they are ready to mate by swimming close together and nuzzling each other. They may do this for more than an hour. The mating process itself lasts less than a minute and is done belly to belly. After mating, the female may become

Dolphins are social creatures and are usually found in groups called pods. The size of a pod ranges from a few dolphins to several hundred.

pregnant. Dolphins usually carry just one baby, which is called a **calf**. Depending on the species, the female will carry the calf inside her body for nine to twelve months.

When the calf is fully developed, the mother dolphin is ready to give birth. She wiggles to push the calf from her body. The calf slips out tail first in a burst of blood. Right away it heads toward the water's surface to take its first breath of air. The mother dolphin helps by gently nudging the calf upward.

The newborn dolphin looks a lot like its parents, only smaller and often with different skin markings and colors. At first the calf's dorsal fin and tail flukes

A dolphin calf swims with its mother. Baby dolphins keep close to their mothers during their first two years.

are floppy, but they become firm within a few days. The calf's brand-new muscles also get stronger as the calf practices its swimming skills. Before long the small dolphin is swimming effortlessly. With a little help from its mother, it manages to keep up with the fully grown members of its pod.

The Baby's Life

A dolphin calf sticks close to its mother. It goes everywhere she goes. It even leaps out of the water whenever the mother does. As baby and mother move from place to place, they "talk" to each other with squeaks, whistles, and clicks. They also rub and touch each other.

For the first six months of its life, a calf eats nothing but its mother's milk. It gets the milk from nipples that are hidden in slits on the mother's belly. Since the calf must surface often to breathe, it nurses for just a few seconds at a time. But those few seconds are enough. Dolphins' milk is very rich. It contains a lot of fat, which helps the baby to form the blubber layer it needs to stay warm. It also helps the baby to grow bigger and stronger very quickly.

Sometime within the first year of its life, a baby dolphin sprouts teeth. After this happens, the young dolphin starts trying solid foods. It gradually

Teeth emerge during the first year of a dolphin's life. Once this happens, the dolphin begins to eat solid food.

eats more and more solids and less and less milk. By the time the calf is two years old, it is weaned. This means it no longer needs its mother's milk. At this point the young dolphin may leave to join another pod. In some species, however, dolphins stay with their birth pods throughout their lives.

Growing Up

A newly weaned calf is not yet an adult. It is still a young dolphin with a lot of growing up to do. Over the next few years the dolphin plays, eats, and learns about life in the sea. Its skin color changes and becomes more like that of an adult. The dolphin also grows larger and stronger.

After several years, a dolphin reaches maturity. This means it is now an adult, able to have babies of its own. The exact timing of adulthood varies from species to species. Some dolphins are considered adults when they are just five or six years old. Others take a few years longer. In most species, females reach maturity earlier than males do.

Dolphins begin mating soon after they reach maturity. The females become pregnant and give birth to calves. They will have a new calf every two to three years for the rest of their lives. Dolphins can live up to forty years, so a particular female may give birth to many calves. Most of these new dolphins will eventually have babies of their own, and the cycle of life will continue.

chapter 3

Catch of the Day

Dolphins are **predators**, which means they hunt and eat other animals. Because dolphins are very active, they must eat a lot of other animals to get the energy they need. An adult gobbles down 4 to 5 percent of its body weight each day.

To find this much food, dolphins spend a lot of time hunting. In the open water, they chase fish, squid, jellyfish, and small swimming shrimp. In shallow water, dolphins may also pluck crabs, clams, and other bottom-dwelling creatures from the ocean floor.

Finding Food

Before a dolphin can eat, it must find food. Dolphins swim gracefully through the sea as they

A dolphin prepares to gobble down a squid for dinner. Because dolphins need to eat a lot for energy, adults spend a great deal of their time hunting for food.

search for prey. They use their sharp eyes to look for tasty animals in the water or on the ocean floor. They also use their echolocation skills. Using their built-in sonar, dolphins can "see" swimming animals as far as one-half mile away. If the creatures seem small enough to eat, the dolphins swim over to get a better look.

Dolphins usually stay near the water's surface when they hunt. If they cannot find anything to eat in shallow waters, however, they may make deep hunting dives. Dolphins can dive to depths of about two thousand feet. In the deep water, hungry dolphins often find a meal.

A hunting dolphin will grab a lone fish if it sees one. But since dolphins travel in large groups, schools of prey are better. A big school of fish or squid can feed an entire pod, not just one dolphin. Pod members spread out so they can search a larger area. When one dolphin spots a school of prey, it calls to the other dolphins. They all swim over quickly. They are ready to feast.

Catching and Eating

After prey is found, it must be caught. Dolphins often work together to catch prey. They surround a school of fish or squid, herding it into a tight ball. Then the dolphins take turns swimming through the trapped school. Because the prey are packed

Dolphins often work together to catch their prey.

together so tightly, they are very easy for the dolphins to catch.

Some scientists believe that dolphins can also stun prey with powerful beams of sound. According to this theory, a dolphin gets close to its prey, then sends out a deafening sound blast. The blast confuses the prey and temporarily ruins its sense of direction. In this confused state, the prey has no chance of escape.

Sharks are one of the ocean's most fearsome predators. Dolphins in a pod are generally safe from sharks.

Dolphins do not always surround or stun their prey. Sometimes they just chase it. Most types of dolphins can swim faster than twenty-five miles per hour for short bursts. This is speedy enough to catch almost any prey animal. When the dolphin gets close enough, it strikes the prey with its powerful tail. It may hit the prey hard enough to throw it into the air. When the stunned fish falls back to the water, the dolphin swims over to claim its meal.

Whatever technique a dolphin chooses, the predator soon gets close to its prey. The dolphin then opens its mouth and bites down on its victim. The prey is held tight by rows of peglike teeth. Depending on the species, a dolphin may have anywhere from 8 to 250 teeth. A dolphin's teeth are not sharp enough to spear prey, but they are very good for grabbing and tearing. They easily rip large prey into bite-sized pieces.

Smaller prey is not usually ripped. The dolphin bites the prey just hard enough to stun or kill it, then swallows it whole. Fish are swallowed headfirst so their bony spines will not snag in the dolphin's throat.

Natural Enemies

Dolphins are not just hunters. They are also hunted by larger animals. Big sharks such as great whites and tiger sharks catch and eat dolphins whenever they can. Smaller dolphins may also be eaten by large dolphins, especially orcas. Very young dolphins, very old dolphins, and dolphins that are sick or injured are most likely to be eaten.

A trainer feeds a dolphin at a tourist camp. Humans are the greatest threat to dolphins in the wild.

Dolphins keep themselves safe by sticking together. Few predators are bold enough to attack a pod of dolphins. If a predator does come near, the dolphins may attack it as a group. Scientists have seen wild dolphins ramming sharks with their snouts. This kind of attack usually drives the shark away.

Humans and Dolphins

Sticking together cannot protect dolphins from their greatest threat: humans. Many dolphins die each year as a result of human fishing activities. This happens partly because dolphins follow fishing boats, feasting on fish they pull from the fishermen's nets. This is an easy way for a dolphin to get a meal, but it is also dangerous. Dolphins can get tangled in fishing nets. When they do, they usually die.

Boats that hunt tuna are especially likely to catch dolphins by accident. Dolphins and tuna hunt the same prey, so they are often found together. In fact, tuna fishermen often look for dolphins leaping at the water's surface. This tells them that tuna are swimming below. When fishermen spot dolphins, they drop their tuna nets. They catch their intended prey—but they often snag a large number of dolphins as well.

Drift nets are another problem. Drift nets are net "walls" that hang vertically in the water. They may be many miles long. Fishermen drop drift nets into the water and let them sit for a few days before reeling them in. The nets snare all kinds of sea creatures, including dolphins. Often the dolphins become trapped underwater, where they cannot breathe. The dolphins drown before the fishermen can release them.

Laws have been passed to protect dolphins. The Marine Mammal Protection Act (MMPA), which went into effect in 1972, makes it illegal to hunt marine mammals in U.S. waters. This act also limits the number of dolphins that can be taken as bycatch (animals accidentally caught while hunting for another species). And regulations exist worldwide to limit the length of drift nets. These regulations and others have greatly reduced the number of dolphins killed by fishermen each year. Experts hope that with care and continued monitoring, worldwide dolphin populations will remain strong and healthy.

chapter 21

Smart Cetaceans

Dolphins have extremely good communication skills, learn difficult tasks quickly, and can recognize themselves in mirrors. They also have very large brains compared to their body size. According to many scientists, these traits show that dolphins are highly intelligent. After humans, in fact, dolphins may be the smartest animals on earth.

Intelligent Communication?

Many researchers have studied dolphin communication. Some experiments seem to show that dolphins can communicate very specific ideas. In one experiment, for example, scientists placed aluminum poles in the water near a small pod of

A dolphin appears to walk by using its tail to push itself along the surface.

bottlenose dolphins. Using underwater microphones, the scientists listened as the dolphins chattered among themselves for several minutes. Eventually one dolphin left the pod and swam over to the poles. He looked at the poles for a while, then returned to the pod. The dolphins chattered some more. Then all the dolphins swam past the poles without hesitation. It appeared that the "scout" dolphin had told the others that the poles were harmless.

In another experiment, scientists taught dolphins to understand a special sign language. The language had about fifty simple words, such as *ball, in,* and *fetch.* Once the dolphins had learned the individual words, scientists combined the words to form commands. The dolphins easily understood the commands. They fetched balls, swam through hoops, and pushed people around in the water exactly as instructed. One dolphin could even obey a command that meant, "Show me something totally new." To do this, the dolphin had to think creatively.

Quick Learners

Scientists have also examined dolphins' incredible learning abilities. Dolphins have been taught to leap high in the air or do flips on command, carry humans on their backs, jump through hoops, swim through mazes while blindfolded, and perform many other tasks. Dolphins learn very quickly, sometimes mastering new skills after just a few tries.

Dolphins can even learn complicated tasks just by watching each other. At one marine park, a dolphin was trained to raise a flag by bumping a ball with its snout. When this dolphin died, another one immediately took over. Even though the new dolphin had never been trained to raise the flag, he did the task perfectly. He had learned this skill by watching the first dolphin perform.

Dolphins seem to enjoy the learning process. A dolphin will work long hours to master a new task. If the dolphin is being lazy, the trainer can "punish" it by walking away from the tank. In response, the dolphin often starts working harder. It acts as if it does not want the training session to end.

Self-Recognition

Self-recognition is another unusual dolphin ability. Dolphins know they are seeing themselves when they look at a mirror. This ability is very rare in the animal kingdom. Besides dolphins, only humans and the great apes (chimpanzees, gorillas, and orangutans) can recognize their reflections.

Until recently, there was no evidence that dolphins could recognize themselves. But in 2001, scientists at the New York Aquarium conducted an experiment with two bottlenose dolphins named Presley and Tab. The scientists used nontoxic ink to

A pair of dolphins jump over their trainers. Because of their high intelligence, dolphins are easily trained to perform such acrobatic tricks.

make black marks on the dolphins' bodies. They put mirrors into the dolphins' tank. Then they waited to see what the dolphins would do.

In trial after trial, the dolphins swam to the mirrors as soon as they were marked. They twisted and turned their bodies so they could see the marks in the mirror. Each paid no attention at all to the other dolphin's ink marks but seemed fascinated by their own. Both Presley and Tab spent long minutes in front of the mirror each time they got a new mark. According to the scientists conducting the experiment, these behaviors proved that the dolphins knew they were seeing their own reflections.

Experts are not sure what this experiment says about dolphin intelligence. Some scientists think

Dolphins are among the few animals that can recognize themselves. Humans and some apes are the only other animals that recognize their reflections.

self-recognition might mean that dolphins are self-aware. In other words, dolphins may know they are individuals, different and separate from other dolphins. So far only humans are known to have this ability, which is often considered a mark of high intelligence.

Big Brains

To get more information about dolphin intelligence, some researchers have studied dolphins' brains. They have looked at a factor called the **brain/body ratio**, which means the weight of the brain in relation to the weight of the body. Some scientists (though not all) believe that the higher the brain/body ratio, the greater the intelligence of the animal.

Scientists studying this factor have discovered that on average, dolphins' brains make up 1.19 percent of their total body weight. This brain/body ratio is very high. It is second only to that of humans, whose brains make up 2.1 percent of their body weight. It is much larger than the brain/body ratio of chimpanzees, which is just 0.7 percent.

Researchers have also examined the dolphin's **cerebral cortex**. The cerebral cortex is the outer layer of the brain that handles thought, learning, creativity, memory, and other advanced functions. In most animals, the cerebral cortex is smooth and small. But dolphins have big, wrinkled cerebral

Although dolphin performances are popular at aquariums and marine parks, even wild dolphins like to perform such tricks as breaching and tail walking.

cortexes, like humans do. Some researchers think that the dolphin's large cerebral cortex could be the sign of an intelligent mind.

Although scientists disagree about the level of dolphin intelligence, most believe dolphins are among the ocean's most intelligent creatures. But no matter what their level of intelligence, one thing is clear: Dolphins are magnificent creatures that fill an important role in the ocean ecosystem.

Glossary

beak: The dolphin's pointed snout.

blowhole: A hole on the head through which the dolphin breathes.

blubber: A thick layer of fat that lies just beneath the dolphin's skin.

brain/body ratio: The weight of the brain in relation to the weight of the body.

breaching: Leaping out of the water.

calf: A baby dolphin.

cerebral cortex: The outer layer of the brain, which handles thought and other advanced functions.

dorsal fin: A triangular fin on the dolphin's back.

drift net: A fishing net that hangs vertically in the water. Drift nets may be many miles long.

echolocation: The ability to "see" with sound. Sound waves are sent out, and the returning echoes are interpreted.

flukes: Flattened pads of tough tissue at the end of the dolphin's tail.

marine mammal: A mammal that lives in an ocean environment.

melon: An oil-filled organ in the dolphin's head that changes and directs sound waves.

migration: An annual movement from one home to another.

pectoral flippers: Two flippers just behind and to the bottom of the dolphin's head.

pod: A group of dolphins.

predator: Any animal that hunts other animals for food.

For Further Exploration

Books

Kathleen Dudzinski, *Meeting Dolphins.* Washington, DC: National Geographic Society, 2000. In this book, a marine biologist describes her career and her work with dolphins. Also includes lots of basic information about dolphins.

Wayne Grover, *Dolphin Adventure.* New York: HarperTrophy, 1990. This book tells the true story of a scuba diver who saves a baby dolphin's life.

Elaine Pascoe, *Animal Intelligence: Why Is This Dolphin Smiling?* San Diego, CA: Blackbirch Press, 1998. This book presents evidence of dolphin intelligence.

Judith Janda Presnall, *Navy Dolphins.* San Diego, CA: KidHaven Press, 2002. Learn how dolphins help the U.S. Navy to rescue people, identify enemy swimmers, and detect bombs and mines.

Websites

David's Whale & Dolphin Watch (neptune.atlan tis-intl.com/dolphins). This site features a wealth of dolphin pictures that can be downloaded and used in school projects.

Dolphin's World (www.dolphinswrld.netfirms. com). This site includes fact sheets on the most common dolphin species as well as dolphin pictures, puzzles, games, screen savers, and more.

Index

picture credits

Cover Photo: Corel

about the author

Kris Hirschmann has written more than ninety books for children. She is the president of The Wordshop, a business that provides a wide variety of writing and editorial services. She holds a bachelor's degree in psychology from Dartmouth College in Hanover, New Hampshire. Hirschmann lives just outside of Orlando, Florida, with her husband, Michael, and her daughter, Nikki.